Hymn for the Black Terrific

HYMN FOR THE BLACK TERRIFIC

POEMS

KIKI PETROSINO

Sarabande Books
LOUISVILLE, KENTUCKY

Managing Editor
Sarabande Books, Inc.
2234 Dundee Road, Suite 200
Louisville, KY 40205

Library of Congress Cataloging-in-Publication Data

Petrosino, Kiki, 1979–
  [Poems. Selections]
  Hymn for the black terrific : poems / by Kiki Petrosino.
    pages ; cm.
  ISBN 978-1-936747-59-7 (pbk. : alk. paper)
  I. Title.
  PS3616.E868H96 2013
  811'.6—dc23
                                    2013005921

Cover image by Philip Miller.
Cover and text design by Sarabande Books.

Manufactured in Canada.
This book is printed on acid-free paper.

Sarabande Books is a nonprofit literary organization.

This project is supported in part by an award from the National Endowment for the Arts.

The Kentucky Arts Council, the state arts agency, supports Sarabande Books with state tax dollars and federal funding from the National Endowment for the Arts.

CONTENTS

TURN BACK YOUR HEAD
& THERE IS THE SHORE   37

For Philip
penman, painter, drawer, limner

画家

I scarcely dared to look
to see what it was I was.

—Elizabeth Bishop

HYMN

FOR THE

BLACK TERRIFIC

OISEAU REBELLE

PERSONAL STYLE MONOLOGUE

The doctor is in. Martinis are out.
Dirty is in. Stripes are out.
Absence is out. Driving is in.
Black lung is in. Angry is out.
Bacon is in. Sparkles are in.
Elbows are in. Wasp waists are in.
Portugal is out. Velveeta is in.
The Strokes are out. Kiss is back in.
Time travel is in. Going out is out.
To be in is out. To be out is still out.
Blondes are in. Blades are in.
Vampires are in. Gullets are out.
The power is out. Darkness is in.
America is out. America is out.
The dark is here.

THIS WOMAN'S FACE IS YOUR FUTURE

I, too, have hated it. Something off about the teeth. Long & long, I've studied on its shape: dumb as domett. Dulsome as Dallas ditchwater. *Lantern-head,* I've said. *Happy horsebag, too bad to bleed.* Just wanna iron shut its mouth from hem to hem. Wanna break the nose down to a hawse-hole. Could I gag it out? Once gagged, I mean, with long dry coughs of hair. Could I shutter it with one quick knot to the nape? Snap it off in my hands? Old blister pack, old zit. In my cabin, I'd snag that thing on the first nail. Keep pulling it down & down by the jaw. Yes, & let them shreds hang lovely in the lamps. Only then would I give up awhile. Put on my sea-gown & rise, beautiful on the dark decks.

ALLERGENESIS

They come in their millions, breaking open in the muck. They come
with their barnacle bodies blooming. In white, in sulfur colonies
they come. Rising from radial engines of dark, from millions of low
hatcheries they come, unfolding their jaws sequin by sequin. They
come hot & star-limbed & buzzing, with their wire bones, with
their names turning edgewise in the mouth. *Bloodweed, Chestbane,*
the names. *Knifeclock, Mulehook,* the names. They come lifting
themselves long as sentences in air, spiraling down the rifled barrel
of the windpipe. Riven & sweltering & swelling, they come into
the body's sad lake, its blue bag of steam. So I, Eater of Pith, I
Gum Knuckles, I, Threshing Spoon, must move in wiles across the
tracheal field, must knock & drag to meet them where they camp,
deep in the soft combs of the lungs. Even my breath turns black as I
pursue my course. See their millions of insectile wings grown thick
with theft. Come, let me clutch at them with my medicine claw &
my blood helmet. Down in the fens of histamine.

OISEAU REBELLE

A sister is the one with claws
of char across her back. Her tongue no
denser than a seed. At night she shines
her small sharp keel of sternum
arc by arc. So I cut her out
with blade & board. Tiny *thrum* of blood
in the treedark.

A SISTER IS A THOUGHT CURVING BACK ON HERSELF

I watch her, small & stepping through dark doors. She wears a skirt stitched from sparrows' ribs & speaks a language dug from the hum of coal tar. Somehow she's grown arms like engines, spinning earth & oxygen from the rain-wet. Her mouth, which once resembled mine, now buckles like the beak of a record player over the blade of her face. She hears not *ginger* or *Beijinger*, though I've transmitted these to her in dozens of pink nacelles. She moves in a wish world, pressing her glass cleats down into the mulch, blistering the daisies in their beds. When I wake up in the small breastbone of night, thinking of her name, the white terrific clock of it—I think of cities made narrow by fire, I think of peacocks moving their slow tongues of ash. *A sister is a thought curving back on herself.* This bruise dazzles.

ANCESTORS

One rages, white as wood.
Another sits ruined at the center of her realm.
One of them broods over a clutch of old combs.
One darkens like an oyster in the autumn smoke.
There's one the shape of a ganglion, & one like a yawl.
There's one climbing up from the deep planks.
You find a glass one. A leather one. A salt one.
You watch one dissolve into the embrace of an oak.
Already there's one drawing a fine grid on your forehead.
There's one disjoining the cables of your wrist.
One lives in horses. Another in a warp of snow.
One's a kind of luster in the mouth. You remember one
who taught you to make a kerchief of your hands.
Another came in a nightdress browned with spit.
Sometimes, you glimpse one moving through the woods.
Or whispering through the slits of an iron rake.
There's one who waits, & one who weeps on the road.
But you choose the one who blooms like a war by night.
The one pulling another sheaf of your hair into her mouth.
That one is always here. That one, that tender
trench knife in the head.

BOOKS

After Gregory Orr

For the Bolt of the Body in the Hinge of the Darker Door.
When the Beloved is a Density of Threads.

Concerning All Ingots, All Hinges, All Belts.
Concerning the Fastness Where the Body Stalks.

For the Fin of White which is the Stalk of the Beloved Body.
Where to Stalk, Where to Ride, Where to Strike.

Where to Strike the Beloved in the Body.
For the Armature that Strikes at the Beloved Dark.

Concerning the Varieties of Striking Sounds in the Body.
For the Beloved Strike that Strikes, Once.

When the Sound of the Beloved is the Wood of the Pear Tree.
Concerning the Tree that Roots in the Beloved Dark.

Concerning the Dark that Branches the Body.
A Sound through the Branches of the Beloved Skin.

When the Braid of the Beloved Brushes the Collarbone.
When the Breath of the Beloved Appears on a Glass.

Beloved Terraces, Beloved Darknesses, Beloved Doors.
Concerning the Door of the Body which is a Body's Breath.

For the Burn of the Body at the Edge of the Door.
Near the Edge of the Body of the Beloved.

A Breath on the Body of the Beloved.
On the Body, which is a Garden of Unfolding Edges.

For the Garden where the Beloved Unfolds.

NOCTURNE

Last night, the one I loved
before you went before me, walking
with his bride.

I followed with my broken
feet & coat unlatched. He called
her *cake* & *coin* & *wing*

& told her of a place so high
the pines grow small
as thumbs.

They went talking into
the trees the wedding trees
the trees   only I

felt the earth a dark
cut on my gums I held
my teeth in such cloud

of grit. *Hosanna.*
Then came I to the brink
of this tower room

where I have watched
the corsair ships, their iron dazzle
like a field of ghosts.

You must never sail from me
into the blind seep of that
blue mist.

I mean to tell you   *no*
in my language, slow
with blood

no   from my cakewhite
belly I say *The night*
is a knife of salt & every star

sleeps on a bed of smoke
yet still you go from me, more gone
than glass, your skin

an acre of tallgrass speeding
behind the window
& the halves of my head

make a hoofbeat
a thing not born, but flooded
with sound—

It's true, it is true

No music
in the world except
what I jaw

& my jaws are black
& fearsome mine.

THE TERRIBLE TEST OF LOVE

If you were scrimshaw, & this the Arctic loop with miles to climb. If I had feet unslippered & a knife. If, in busted crenellations of my teeth there kept a knife. Such knife there kept. Such colored *if,* that knife. If kept the colored *if* of knife, the colored feet, & kept a folio behind a door outsized. My will to touch, outsized, that colored *if.* My will outsized, to touch the naked seabass of such knife. My colored teeth, my swarms. If you, my scrim, my awl, behind a door should sleep, & then—if I should come, in swarms of dark? O love, to climb that Arctic loop of dark, to best that door, to swarm. If I should cross that only door? My only love, my best. If you should wake from tuneless dark & call *O best, best, O most best,* my knife unslippered at the door, my naked will outsized. What answer then? What seabass clangs in tuneless *I*? Pull back, pull back, my crenellated arms. Pull back, my naked feet, outswarmed. My Arctic will behind a seabass door creeps back inside the clanging room of loops. Where sleeps my only love, keep *I* awake with crenellated cry. Where *loop, loop, loop, loop* is tuneless in the folio of night.

ALVERTA

Say she was noble: a bright & foreign kind. Her long-gloved hands, her smell of coins & salt. She had a way of staring over the yokes of trees at you. Slim, in her woven skirt & church heels. All that light hair twisting through a comb like speech. Now say the railroad came & changed the whole county. Railroad came & slithered over the mountains to where you can't catch. Tobacco in the lungs, grease unfolding in the mouth. How, year by year, your father's voice grew narrower. *Clifton*, he called you. *Butler-William-Henry*. Back to the home-place where God lay like a spine in the earth. But say you kissed her, once: a taste of glass. Say she muttered over you. Grandfather of smoke, grandfather of great sorrow. Tell us what you gave for all the stars drowned in her skin. For her womanish back of the neck, tilting away.

HYMN FOR THE BLACK TERRIFIC

*

With this spell, I conjure you.
I draw your lazy bullets through my head.
A little smoke, a little bone dust. My grin a kayak
balanced, balancing.

It takes a kayak of blood to raise a devil.
Rotting robe of mallow stems. Belt of lion's hair.
I'll stand here in your magic swamp til the myrrh
dries in my mouth.

You say: *Some things get denser in the dark.*
I only spit & snag. Dream of ocean kayaks, crisp
as canapés. All night, your long teeth test me.
Long nips at the ridge of my jaw. *Soon,* you say.

But in the woods, I comb your secret smoke
into kayak-shapes. My hands go dark with craft.
Maybe I'm your mother, pushing off from shore.
Watch me whittle, rib by rib.

I'm hulled like hell's own ship. Bite down
to find my skin's been hammered through.
So what? Here's a cottonfish, sunk in an old kayak.
We're drifting on the dead

but I've built you something bloody
with the blades of my hands.
Come & roost here. It's full dark.
Nothing good can get me off.

Here's a nook for my black blade.
Here's the swamp I've scraped in my head.
Come & roost here, with your rotting robe.
You kayak-shape, you key.

Bite down, if you want. It's full dark.
A little smoke twists through the swamp.
I feel your old jaws snag on the stem of a grin.
Soon, you say. Teeth plated with weeds.

A swamp is a lonely billet. All night, I drift
& the starlit world goes dense with bone dust.
Are you my son? Are you my smallest rib?
It takes a rake of blood to reach you.

Even my sleep goes dark & swampish now.
Even my arms, dense as mallow stems.
In the disk of the woods, in the comb of the pines
I spit & I jaw. I spit & jaw & call.

But no spell draws you in. No sweet fin
comes near. You're dear to me as sleep or fire.
You scissor-jaw. I spit & starve
til I'm sick with sensing you.

Maybe you're a cottonfish, conjuring in myrrh.
Sweet words threaded through your thumbnail-skull.
Only let me nip at you with my long teeth.
Some things get denser in the dark.

*

In the dream of swamps, I'm a woman
with a knife. Thin belts of color on the blade.
Some things get denser here. Some scales
peel back like sequins from the eyes.

A woman is a lordly thing. Hard as belts.
Mean as cat dirt in the dark. A woman rakes
herself down to the girders. A little air
seeps in, a little smoke & buzz.

Some say I'm a woman. Some call me so.
No matter what, I just get handsomer.
Count my ribs. Now count my belts of fat.
Only one of us can get off. Guess who?

You talk, mallow-mild. I must've built you
from a kit. So fast your teeth fit the marks
in my head. *Soon* you say. But what
does it mean to bite down in the dark?

I'm here for your headful of animal sounds.
You said to draw a diamond in the air & wait.
You lion claw. Come see what I've digged
with the teeth of my face.

RAGWEED

Neither wax, nor egg, nor honey on the knife.
In garden not, nor street nor bus nor bank—
Not sleep. Not word. Nor will-over-will
Not lung. Not hull, or sail. Just crank & tread

in place [no place] & white [not white] gets hot
& seethe & seethe—my sleep like steam
not long, but less. So less, till I am I who cracks
at last, begs *air* & says *Am I such root? Such rot*

for rage who scrapes, who darks each swatch of flesh
each branch of mesh & salt & bit? This rag—it rob
& sneak & rob & sneak, my tongue gets pins & pine & less
& less. Can run, but run gets gone. Can bellow, bellow

change. Only *most,* only *half,* & less & less get
here, get thick & stick. Not breath.

ADVISORY PROTOCOL

Remember that it is not your responsibility to account for the severely troubled. You need only swallow enough needles & enough bread. The first disruption will resemble a silver collapse of the inner ear. Then it enters the room. In such cases, you must hold yourself in a state of tonic immobility, letting your remaining teeth fall to the carpet. If you find yourself shrinking to the thinness of a soap leaf, if you perceive your tongue halting in its progress across the windowpane, you may have entered a rare or acute oscillation. Try to exit firmly & with respect. In this, mark your training. Mark that each of your hands is a perianth of light. Where you wanted to go can't be reached by lip-gloss anymore. Get up, get up. You'll have to climb.

AT THE TEAHOUSE

I can't understand anything with this mud
& the pieces of silk & peacocks singing. Here's a whole
farm painted orange on a Thursday, & here's a tricycle
at the brink of a scream. I have things, like the sugar jones
I can't help bringing to every lunch. This village is rad & huge
as smoke. Look at my flat gold feet chattering over mucky stacks
of tiles. No one yells at me in the light. Once upon a time
I had enough anger in me to crack crystal. I boiled up from bed
in my enormous nightdress, with my lungs full of burning
chrysanthemums. Now just imagine the color of the sky
in my braincase. I'm drinking tea with diamonds in it.
My blood cells race like star-clawed kites over every knuckle
of the roof of this pavilion. Everyone I've loved is balanced
on the edge of my chopstick. I lean back to yell for *the sun the sun*
the sun the sun the sun—& a small cup of tea arrives
whose Chinese name is "Pieces of Shreddedness." Dear Mother
yesterday love was a rockery of accumulated refinement, & today
it's a donkey named Goodbar dipping out from a doorway. I can't
simmer down, & I won't simmer down. Some people make
a life of straw. Some people get holy
on not much at all.

POSTCARD FROM OGUN STATE

They tell me not to wander alone in this hotel, but to me an unseen moon is a dead face going nowhere. In the half-dark, a single bat surges across the corridor: a punctuation mark in the shape of a swing, a silence with a hot light in it. I've never seen a bat before & then I have. I've never seen rain dropping hard through a hole in a cloth umbrella, & then a driver picks me up for dinner in the rain. I'm brought to the Pepper Soup Arena in a black car, & more rain pummels & smears the windows, one by one. I understand *corridor*, I understand *dinner*, as a kind of ground I cross with caution in the dark. I get out, I get out. There's a trench at the edge of every door. At the brink of each trench, another brink, & then a border sharpened with stockade fencing. Whole neighborhoods close themselves, as if with belts. Freshly tapped, the palm wine in my calabash is more ruthless than beer. It gets away from me, fast. They say to proceed with caution through each plate, as if the table were a field alive with birds & tall grasses. But I get lost among the starches, in the blood-deep venison that keeps appearing on my tongue. I can't stop looking down, into the floor's wet. So this is what I've been tilting at, for so long. This is the face I've asked to see.

CYGNUS CYGNUS

For Dean Young

To love a theory leaves no room for imprecision. Let us count:
Here is a king. Here is a catfish. Here is a staff of office.
Here's a sad-beaked animal nibbling at my poor snack cake of grief.

Hello, sad animal. Turns out, you're not making the swim back.
Pythagoras argued that the souls of poets pass not from this world
but lodge themselves in the breastwork of swans.

Let it be, then. Let some of us withdraw to the keel-shaped bones
to the tilted orrery of the thorax. But I think: if poets coalesce as swans
we're mostly in the feet of swans, black as drums

pressing our rageful webbing into the earth's flank.
The sound of a swan is no chemical thing, but a bloody hum
thick with rivalry & blue weather. It's rage that moves

the tongue of a swan in strange meters, it is only rage
that pulls the tarsometatarsus back to the joint, like
a bowstring stretched to the edge

of its hungry self. Just so, you taught me to be warlike
in my songs & still to praise the palm-sized stars
brooding over their great darkness.

I see how *art* is. It's a fine blast furnace, & my knuckles
make an imperfect pomegranate-delivery system. It's tempting
to lie to the young. But you told us rightly about the beautiful

dead flamingoes holding up the continent, & the thousands
of microscopic bluebirds who once pinned the canopy of Iowa
in place. Last time I passed your house, something with a beak

& wings had pecked a line of punctuation in the stucco
then dressed each small exit with a different, loosening fist
of dry grass. I wanted to tell you: *The neighborhood is full*

of unusual craft today, professor. But instead, I let the moon
swing like a lantern over the old, sugary architecture
of your road. To be a poet is to surface plainly

from the wound of sleep. To observe how thickly feathered
the heart, how small & bright the planet of human thought.
When you tell the sky goodbye in your poems

it's awful. Every time. This last lesson moves beyond
my study. But you remain with me as a winter sky
shot through with swans of iron, swans of steel.

Let no harm come to the dark you have made.

MULATTRESS

Misery is often the parent of the most affecting touches in poetry. Among the blacks is misery enough, God knows, but no poetry.

—Thomas Jefferson, *Notes on the State of Virginia*

[1]

What would you trade *they*
ask, if you could trade for beauty? If you could *secrete*
or slice or tender an exchange? A little *less by*
this business of poetry, they ask; rather, *the kidneys*
cut into bright arcs, plated with care *& more*
vivid now because divorced from your body? If, *by the glands*
you could alter your person, strip your skull *of the skin*
& imagine the eye's dry orbital a window *which gives*
onto your grandmother's terrace (full of pigeons look at *them*
million wings burning)? If you could become *a very strong*
horizon made crisp with towers *&*
huge stones, would you slip your *disagreeable*
knot of flesh, then, O apple of dark, *O Door?*

[2]

My mother, with legs like a deer. How *they*
carry her slimwise in winter. Her *secret*
name. Her holy shape. Always, she's *less by*
than with, or near to me. Like *the kidney-*
shaped sadness I carry in my head, *& more*
brightening ever. You can read *by the glands of the skin*
how she knitted me. I love her hands, *which*
lift into sudden lakes. In Baltimore, all water *gives*
itself to *them*
that's brave enough to walk on ice. *A very strong*
mother like mine walks by *& disagreeable*
ice weeps itself to mud. Sometimes I catch my mother
in a handful of mint, its *odor*
fresh as stars.

[3]

I didn't know my color till *they*
called me by its dirty name: a coin *secrete*d
in the body's bank. Now I move *less by*
gathering names to swelter in *the kidneys*
or in the lake behind my teeth, *& more*
electric-wise, crackling in air. I can show you *by the glands*
how I surpass my proofing dish. *Of the skin*
there's nothing more to confess, a fact *which gives*
me leave to sing. I want to tell *them: A*
colored body confirms a bridge, *very strong*
across the synapses *& disagreeable*
to caliper. Still, between us, this human *odor.*

[4]

A colored body is a wreck *they*
rake with a strobe light. All its *secret*
halls & winking panes. We know it *less by*
& by, a sunk ballroom. How *the kidneys*
weep in their niches *& more*
holy grow every hour. We measure beauty *by the glands*
or by the clear metronome *of the skin.*
It's only beauty *which gives*
us pause. But I love *them a*
little more who love me from the *very*
bolts. Myself: slewfooted, *strong & disagreeable.*
Iron in the head. Iron, my *odor.*

[5]

I want to talk about your house, how *they*'ve
painted it 'oyster white.' As if home were a pearl *secrete*d
about the sand-grain of your bed. You speak *less by*
the declarations of the body (*the kidneys*
& the red-gold gallop of your tongue) *& more*
by your French partitioned doors. When I walk *by the*
library, even your chair turns its spine. My fabulous *glands*
weep a little, under the arms. Strange how the cabinet *of the skin*
you hardly registered, until you did. *Which gives*
me such a headwound. When I think of all *them*
crystal tumblers nobody'll ever use again, *a very strong*
loneliness takes me up. You're so sharp *& disagreeable*
to hold. *Je t'adore.*

[6]

I don't trust this body *they*
wrap like a razor blade in *secret*
crinolines. They want me blood*less*
& soft in the jaws. Can't recall *by the*
boudoir light how it felt to have little-*kid knees*
like moons in the dark, to have h*and*s
alive with sweat & lightning bugs. I'm a *Moor*
now, I'm a Moor. You can tell *by the glance*
I use to trouble grown-up men. *Of the skin*
I've got two square yards & a sob. They say a *witch*
dug me up from a barrow. I *gives them a*
smile at that. It's true, my color's *very strong*—
a high *& disagreeable*
gold. You can't enter a hall with n*o door.*

[7]

My colored body is so clean *they*
ask to run their fingers over the *secret*
songlines on my scalp. I crunch on the harm*less*
glitter left by their love of me. By & *by*
I've seeped onto every flatscreen. I'm *the kid*
with a talent. Spokesmodel. Young attor*ney.*
Kid, I'm beautiful. Look at my televised h*and*s
pale & polished; they peel in the sun like syca*more*s.
But: a Florentine once confessed, *by the*
light of a lake, that he'd never marry me. To *glance*
yes, of course, but not to marry. He said: *'Of the*
women I know, you are not of my future.' Without *skin*
there's little point to love, or roast duck. *Which*
I learned by trying each thing both ways. It *gives*
me headaches to explain myself abroad. To *them*
I'm some dark hatchway, viewed from *a very*
high window. Storybook-*strong &*
carved all over in some *disagreeable*
dialect. Who doesn't love a sealed corr*idor?*

[8]

Mother says I came from angels. *They secrete*d
a warning in my skin. When I wear this back*less*
gown, it glows. The angels wrote: '*By the*
buzz of the sea, by brake & by s*kid*
by darkness of ho*ney &*
by moth-shade shall she weep.' *More*
than this, Mother didn't tell. So I learned to *bite the*
heads off snakes & wander all the clangin*g lands of*
Other. A huntsman gave me a bangle that burned *the skin*
on my arms. In the woods, a *witch*
tried to seal me up in an oak. I learned to for*give them*
all with my bare hands. This body makes *a very strong*
sort of gunlock now. Mother, I travel dark *& disagreeable*
in my own country. No sound is my ambass*ador.*

[9]

I live in a country *they*
didn't leave for me. My color *secrete*s
like taffy through my pores, or should. But I'm *less*
polite when pulled. Try to tell *by the kidneys*
where I'm from, or who made me, *& more*
lunatic moths race *by.*
Do you think *the glance*
of a colored woman is a glitch *of the skin*
or the proof of a *witch*?
No one for*gives*
me for sitting beside *them*
at lunch or for wearing *a very strong*
set of thighs. In this country, we're all sad *& disagreeable*
to each other. Someone, open *a door.*

[10]

They're blessed, who made me. *They*
who gave me lungs & life. Who mixed, in *secret*
centuries, by garden-light, in weight*less*
air, who mixed in air made weightless *by the*
shades of touch. Who set my *kidneys &*
my bones like beryls. Who sketched my hairline *more by*
love than math. Who tuned *the glands*
& strung the veins along my legs, are blessed *of*
me, they're blessed. I must bless *the skin*
I carry through this dark. I bless this dark, *which*
carries on for miles. Those fathers, I *give them*
back their tractors of light. To those mothers, I give *a*
cabin, bright with breath. For e*very strong &*
sullen pull of this blood, I crown their sweet *disagreeable*
names with heli*odor.*

TURN BACK YOUR HEAD
& THERE IS THE SHORE

The Dark could not perceive its own form
It was not a silk to be worn.

—Alice Notley

EATING HOUSE

We begin with artichokes. Blade by blade. Two closed fists & a skirt planed with pleats. Where the eater half-stands among kitchen plants. She, too, wants a baby. She, too, is sick with blades. Her hips clasp over her old inward choke, the dull, dumb buds. Not reached by ringing, they, & she has rung. Rung & scratched & not been sent for. She thinks: *Time oldens.* Artichokes babble on their fleshy necks. It's lonely here, isn't that true? Scratching in the garden like a hen, & like a hen she *oldens,* the cords in her throat divide with want. A baby wants front teeth & silk-patched pillows, a baby does. Isn't that true? The eater has a brain full of broth. She is wearing boiled cloth. Straight from the bolt. The broad.

SUPER MILK FLAVOR

Lately, the eater has begun to eat again. Egg yolks, guar gum. Buttermilk solids spooned up from the pot. She shovels as if there were a medal for shoveling the mounds & mounds of sweetened matter. (*There is*). At the battle of First Manassas, they brought picnics to the field. They brought ladies in thousand-pound dresses to stake down the slopes with their tuffets. Their arms: cakesoft inside the fragile bulbs of sleeve. Then, sweetness was a fine thing, measured in earbobs & applejack. Just as each army attacked with two columns, you couldn't eat with your gloves on, nor have a tongue like the eater's, roughened on peanut gravel & threads of desiccated coconut. Now the eater tastes her own blood & understands the word *abundance* for the first time. It is salt & metal, it is the pulse of lecithin in the curve of every heaped spoonful. Happy is that eater, happy is she who bringeth to her maw the thousands & ten thousands.

DESTINY COMES TOGETHER AS A COLD PLATE

The eater is lonely, so the eater eats. The huge white shark of her skull sallies forth across the teeming table. Bleached as wool the eye that broods, for a time, over tangles of microgreens, over thin scrapes of scallion. The eater breathes a muddy testament into the slaw. She's slow to sink, a catamaran turning on her hulls. In the East, where rivers fork into little cuts, where camels go vanishing down each rib of dirt, love is a rumor licking the eater's neck. There are halls in her head where a man might say his pilgrim name, where he might leave treasures & monuments. Even the lips of him. Even the cheeks. Such a man might carry through, like the scent of woodsmoke in a glove. It could happen.

TURN BACK YOUR HEAD & THERE IS THE SHORE

Not by sailfish alone shall the eater live. This morning, she shuts herself in the galley & uses a flat knife to plate her own tongue in white fondant. This new tongue far surpasses the old: ballast-heavy & warm against the teeth. The bridge deck of her mouth buckles down with it. The eater feels like a music-box tune, weepful & thin. She is whittling down, as they say. Smiling out from darkness. Someone has decorated this whole entire ballroom with fairy lights, & it's summer now on the salt-planked sea. The eater descends a spiral staircase, tugging off one satin glove. How easeful it is below. *When lights go out, experiments go on* says the captain, bowing from his glimmering waist. His face resembles the wood of the pear tree. The eater threads her bare forearm through the crook of his elbow. Together they listen to the cellists drawing their bows across marzipan cellos. A kiss before midnight is all it will take to turn the eater into foam. In the ocean, there are no window seats, no aisles, no seats together, no bulkhead seats, no seats.

TOP OF A DUMPLING, TOP OF A TEMPLE

The mind of an eater is dark as drink. On market day, she moves like an ocean liner among the cases of edible silver leaf & grilled seahorses. How the hull of her chest tips, tenderly, toward the lovely lake of eating sounds. Her hunger is a metallic swish, is the hook in her clanging mouth, which she fills now with the flesh of spider crabs & wild vegetables. *Bell, bell, bell, bell* her lips & teeth repeat, twenty-seven times before swallowing, & again she takes up the fried bread, the shredded beef & mooncake. Each bite exactly as it surfaces before her, each bite a small hotness matched with a saltness & touched to the brightness of near lights. The lights do near. Buildings advance inward on their wooden stilts. The eater's lucky tongue gets freighted, gets flat; her lucky hands fill up with friends. Yes & why shouldn't friends come calling? Why shouldn't she lick them up from her palms? The eater ranges, blackly. Her harp is a harp of blood.

THE PEACEFUL HEART HAS NO HANG-UPS

The eater returns to the municipal garden & sees that it's empty. She remembers just this: two chairs under the willow tree & matching bowls of cold, sweet soup. Then: his long body against the armature of his motorbike, & how he'd first happened to her, in front of the National Library, in view of the exact bend in the river where he would later hand her five white roses once, & once only. The soup contained pale clouds of swiftlet's nests, which she pulled with a large, shallow spoon. Then, too, he had reached into her robe, & she'd let it fall open to the spring air. He was telling her that one of the stars above their heads was not just a star; it was a beautiful gold cylinder with astronauts breathing inside it. His tongue flickered against her teeth, saying the secret names of things: *fairy floss, watermelon seeds*. It was difficult not to think of love as music in the mouth. A small, hot star came to rest inside her ribs, & she called the name, dissolving as she went.

I SHALL ABSORB WHATEVER COMES MY WAY

If this is what it takes to feel better, then the eater will feel something else. She lets her shadow climb like clematis over the mullioned windowglass. Some time ago, she scraped her head against the sideboard & now she can smell daylight coming in. If that's daylight spilling down the edges of her jaw. If that's a star of salt exploding at her temple. Daylight is orange oil & cornflakes, herself in a fresh cabana shirt & trousers on that one vacation by the sea. White hat on the bureau top. Coffee from an envelope. Young rice growing in long stitches over the soaked ground, if that *was* the ground, in dense layers of red like the meat of a star-shaped animal. She bought ropes of tiny shells to wind about her neck & hands. Like any good eater, she cherishes her hands, holding them up to the sides of her face. Those same hands once entered the mouth of a bronze boar, once rubbed its heavy tongue with a coin for luck. If you can taste that coin on your own tongue, if it comes to you in a flash of sweat & patinated grit, it means you'll return to the square where men go ladling long scarves of tripe from their pots & the old boar sits brooding over his sewer grate. You'll bring the hungry spoon of your face to the brink of the serving dish, & what will happen to you then?

NO BIRTH, NO DEATH

Who can say how the eater began? That ugly pinch in the gut, that taste of tungsten on the hands. They say she chose dominion over the inner world. Talking through the hulls of trees. Moving backward by half-lives. She has marked the spines of leaves, the dark undersides of sea-bells she has painted shut. Her heart is a mirror built from ash. Her face is a map made crisp with blood. To catch her, you must keep a doll's diet: four sips of milk & just enough oil to coat the spoon. Hold yourself long as a rifle, moving quickly from road to road. Don't ask for quarter in the houses of the living, or load down your flesh with forage. Contamination begins in the mouth. If the mouth offends, it must burn.

LINKED TO BLOOD

Where is home for an eater? For she fashions neither scrape nor sett. She bowers not, nor tunnels through the earth. The eater drags no egg to her thin sleeping mat of reeds & ruined silk. She lies not on her belly in the dark, nor does she rock in place beneath a scrim of rotting leaves. She renounces all holes & pockets, all dips & divots she denies. The eater packs tight her teeth in the barrel of her braincase, comes out at night to patrol the sharp edges of herself. Her claws push hard at scattered bits of gravel & snapped feathers. They say the world was full of eaters, once: heavy as sea glass, slow as blood. They raked their shadows like wet sheets over the land, brooding in shallow pools, in dense twists of sweet flag. They say those eaters hung like jewels in the quiet swamps. Each face a calm expanse of dotted swiss. Each limb an ingot weighed down with stars. But this eater walks & moves with a cold scorch mark in her belly. Her skin breaks out in tiny polyps. No one blesses her as she comes through the trees, conjuring in her strange mathematics. What is it she knits with the clicking of her tongue? The eater has compound eyes. The eater is a dark pendant.

CROSSING THE BRIDGE

When the eater dreams, she dreams of horses. Surging up from the far grasslands of her ribs, seething across her throat's crescent. She burns her dream-tongue on the smell of them: black as engine grease, sharp as switch cane in the mouth. White horse, yellow horse, horse with hunger in its kick, horse with teeth of blood & foam. Blight Horse, Soon Horse, Horse of Oil, Horse of Dirt & Hair & Windows Breaking. How the eater's head fills up with storms of speeding animals, how they beat their hooves with rage of her. Awake, the eater scrapes her hair into a nest, tries to cough the horse-taste from her throat. Nothing rings against the sink but sound. By now, the eater can't keep from eating. All day, she pushes bread & birds down her gullet, she cuts her lips on half-grilled cactus. Her mind goes bright & strange as the meat of an egg. Is the eater a special girl? She is, she is. A Queen of Flesh & Plants, tall in the torso & famished from fang to forelock. Never full, though her gut hangs heavy in the dark of her dress, though her thighs press together like prayer. Her hate is a hooved body galloping down halls of dust. She grows round & rounder with each white step.

MUSHROOM GROWING BENEATH THE TREE

After Elizabeth Bishop

The eater scarcely reckons what it is she is. Double drumsticks, belly belt. She scarcely stomachs her own skin, off-color & channeled through with caterpillar scars. How she always smells of care-home lavender & something else beneath—a melting pinkness, a rotten spot. Mornings she wakes up later & later, wearing a dumb-calf look she can't help. It sticks like slop to the slats of her skull. If she could fang her own hide open, she'd do it shred by shred. First, the film around her mouth would split & draw away from chin & neck, down breasts grown thin & webby in the light. Suddenly, from Inside, would come an *O!* of pain: the eater's voice, fresh as ozone on her tongue.

I LOVE YOU, NO DISCUSSION

The eater cannot say that she is unwell. Her judgment is bone-dark & edged in deep serrations. When she goes to the mirror, each of her defects surfaces like oil ready to be skimmed. She need only wait for the process to start itself, a blank *click* in the mind. A scissoring through. At such times, the eater gives herself over to the long register of unfolding measurements, the drifting canticle of names & weights. The afternoon ticks down in precisely plated sections. Certain densities in her must bear elimination. All overgrowth must be scraped down to the quick. An age of offerings to clear the core contaminants, to make of each rib a holy lamp. The eater balances on the half-moons of her heels. Tries to visualize the clear ledge of her clavicle rising up like bottle-glass. She's getting old in layers. Look at her neck, loose as a sun-ray in a child's drawing. Look at all that skin, cryptically colored, beginning to pleat at the eyes. For it is written: *the burners of the eyes shall shine like frost. The burners of the eyes shall be chalk-pure.*

MOON-WRAPPED FRAGRANT SPARERIBS

Happy is that eater who rules by the cyclone of her face. By the syrup of her eye shall she drown the clanging earth. For the eater combs justice like beeswax through her hair, & her hands catch only righteousness in their fiery mesh. Therefore, lament neither the appetite that dismasts your cities, nor the emerald in her gut that spins. I tell you, the eater is more terrible than all your needlework of lemongrass, purer than aluminum the eater's hum at eventide. Fear not her blue-black shadow as she cruises into your airspace. There's lightning in the matrix of her marrow. Her teeth make mirrors of the sea.

HERD GIRL'S FAVORITE FLOWER

It's high time for the eater to put on her wedding head & roar at the stars that cinch the sky. Ding-dong for diamond rings & sweet white peonies, ding-dong for breakfasts built & buttered by the pound. A wedding's quick work for any foam-hipped bride, for any bride with thrusters & a tractor voice. Who says the eater must halve herself to heave through lace & eyelets? Let her be large & engaged to anything with blood in it. Shall she marry? Yes, down to her last atom. Shall she travel on the sea? Yes, & her huge parasol shall break like chitin in her jaws. See how she chomps through trash & tempests, how she gallops toward the next good time. Her bridegroom? Rather her sea-shanty. Rather her opera, agog with gongs. Here she plummets, my hearties. The very world's reversed.

EIGHT RENUNCIATIONS OF THE LOOKING-GLASS

Inside every eater is another eater who rejoices backward.
If the eater rejoices, then she does it with her teeth & insect face.
You may rapidly divide any face by honey, by silk, or by wire.
Divided, the loaf of the face cleaves unto the eater & the rest hangs.
Divided or hanged, the eater seethes with blessedness.
Just watch her sweep like a matador through the sickroom.
Blessed, blessed eater with skin like fiberglass & big wishes!
It's most difficult to live on batter. Or not to.

NOTES

The phrase, "the black terrific," comes from a description of Ahab in Herman Melville's *Moby Dick*.

The poem, "At the Teahouse," is dedicated to the singers of Xiaoshuijing village, Fumin County, Yunnan Province.

The *Oxford English Dictionary* defines mulattress as "a woman with one black and one white parent." The word is of 17th-century French derivation and is no longer used today.

The italicized words in the "Mulattress" poems come from a line in Thomas Jefferson's *Notes on the State of Virginia*, Query 14: "They secrete less by the kidneys, and more by the glands of the skin, which gives them a very strong and disagreeable odor." Where appropriate, I have chosen sound over strict sense (e.g., "glands" becomes "glance").

In "Mulattress [5]," the term "oyster white" refers to the special shade of paint used for interior rooms at Monticello.

The poems in the "eater" series are inspired by the names of dishes served to me during recent trips to mainland China. Several titles come directly from the English-language menu of Pure Lotus Restaurant in Beijing. Other titles were taken from food stall menus or are my own fabrications.

The poem, "Eight Renunciations of the Looking-Glass," owes much to Lewis Carroll's *Journeys in Wonderland*.

ACKNOWLEDGMENTS

Many thanks to the editors of the following publications, where versions of these poems first appeared:

91st Meridian: "Postcard from Ogun State"

Bat City Review: "I Shall Absorb Whatever Comes My Way," "Crossing the Bridge"

Black Clock: "Top of a Dumpling, Top of a Temple," "The Peaceful Heart Has No Hang-Ups"

The Chronicle of Higher Education: "Ragweed"

Forklift, Ohio: "Personal Style Monologue," "At the Teahouse," "Cygnus Cygnus"

Gulf Coast: "Super Milk Flavor," "Turn Back Your Head & There is the Shore"

Jubilat: "Alverta"

The New York Times: "Allergenesis"

Tin House: "Moon-Wrapped Fragrant Spareribs," "I Love You, No Discussion"

UNSTUCK: "Ancestors"

The following poems appeared in *The Dark is Here,* a chapbook published by Forklift, Inc. in 2011: "Books," "Nocturne," "The Terrible Test of Love," "A Sister is a Thought Curving Back on Herself," "Advisory Protocol," "At the Teahouse," "Postcard from Ogun State," and "Ragweed."

The poem "Nocturne" appeared under a different title in the collaborative exhibition and commemorative book, *HANNAH,* organized by the University of Iowa School of Art and Art History in 2010.

The poem "Oiseau Rebelle" was published as a limited-edition broadside by the SOON Series at Cornell University in 2010.

The poem "Hymn for the Black Terrific" was commissioned as part of the collaborative exhibition, *Hail Satan*, organized by the Art Academy of Cincinnati in 2011.

Heartfelt thanks to the University of Louisville (in particular, the Department of English and the College of Arts and Sciences), the Bureau of Educational and Cultural Affairs at the U.S. Department of State, the Chinese Writers Association, and the International Writing Program at the University of Iowa for their generous support of portions of this work. Matt Hart, Christopher Merrill, Edward Carey, Xi Chuan, Lisa Russ Spaar, Leslie Jamison, Jin Renshun, Dan Rosenberg, Becca Myers, Kate Thorpe, Isaac Sullivan, Mary Hickman Fernandez, Robert Fernandez, Erina Harris, Callie Garnett, Gregory Lawless, Youngsoon Chon, Andrew Moeller, and Avery Slater offered me their time, hospitality, and inspiration during the writing process. Thank you.

KIKI PETROSINO was born in Baltimore and received her BA from the University of Virginia. She spent two years teaching English and Italian at a private school, after which she earned graduate degrees from the University of Chicago and the Iowa Writer's Workshop. Her debut collection, *Fort Red Border* (Sarabande, 2009) was praised by *The Believer* and shortlisted for the 2009 *Foreword* Book of the Year in Poetry. In 2011, her poem, "Allergenesis," was featured in the Op-Ed section of *The New York Times*. Other poems have appeared in *Tin House, FENCE, jubilat, Gulf Coast,* and elsewhere. Petrosino is the co-editor of *Transom,* an independent online poetry journal and she teaches creative writing at the University of Louisville.